Laws Criminalizing Apostasy in Selected Jurisdictions

Afghanistan • Algeria • Bahrain • Brunei • Egypt • Indonesia • Iran • Iraq • Jordan
Kuwait • Lebanon • Libya • Mauritania • Morocco • Oman • Pakistan • Qatar •
Saudi Arabia • Sudan • Syria • Tunisia • United Arab Emirates • Yemen

May 2014

The Law Library of Congress, Global Legal Research Center
(202) 707-6462 (phone) • (866) 550-0442 (fax) • law@loc.gov • http://www.loc.gov/law

Laws Criminalizing Apostasy in Selected Jurisdictions

Afghanistan • Algeria • Bahrain • Brunei • Egypt • Indonesia • Iran • Iraq • Jordan
Kuwait • Lebanon • Libya • Mauritania • Morocco • Oman • Pakistan • Qatar •
Saudi Arabia • Sudan • Syria • Tunisia • United Arab Emirates • Yemen

Contents

Laws Criminalizing Apostasy in Selected Jurisdictions

Hanibal Goitom, Foreign Law Specialist (Coordinator),
with the Staff of the Global Legal Research Center

I. Comparative Summary

This report surveys the apostasy laws of twenty-three countries in Africa, the Middle East, South Asia, and Southeast Asia. The survey primarily focuses on jurisdictions that make apostasy a capital offense. However, several countries that have adopted broadly-defined laws on blasphemy and insult to religion, which could potentially be used to prosecute persons for apostasy, have also been included, as well as one country that expressly prohibits extrajudicial punishment for allegations of apostasy.

The countries surveyed that expressly make apostasy a capital offense are Afghanistan, Brunei, Mauritania, Qatar, Saudi Arabia, Sudan, the United Arab Emirates, and Yemen. However, only a small number of cases showing the application of these capital punishment laws were identified. Only two cases were identified that resulted in conviction for religious conversion—one in Iran in 1994 and another in Sudan in 2014. The country surveys also indicate that apostasy laws are frequently used to charge persons for acts other than conversion. For example, in Mauritania, Saudi Arabia, Jordan, and Yemen, individuals were charged with apostasy for their writings or comments made on social media. Of the countries researched, it appears that Iran is the only one that has executed a person convicted of apostasy to date.

It is important to note that in many jurisdictions where apostasy is a capital offense, sentencing is conditional on the defendant's behavior once he is charged or convicted. For instance, in Afghanistan, Brunei, Sudan, and Yemen, a conviction for apostasy can be vacated if the defendant denounces his new faith and rejoins Islam. In Mauritania, a person brought on charges of apostasy is given an opportunity to repent both before and after his conviction. If the person repents after his conviction, the country's Supreme Court can dramatically reduce his sentence.

In some places, such as Saudi Arabia, the criminalization of apostasy is a result of the wholesale adoption of Sharia'a (Islamic law). In most of the countries that make apostasy a capital offense the crime is made part of the countries' penal code either directly or by reference. For instance, the offense is part of Mauritania's 1983 Criminal Code, the United Arab Emirates' Penal Code of 1987, Sudan's Penal Code of 1991, Yemen's Penal Code of 1994, Qatar's 2004 Penal Law, and Brunei's 2013 Criminal Code (however, in Brunei the provision on apostasy is not yet in force). Afghanistan and Qatar have incorporated the crime of apostasy into their criminal laws by reference to what are known as the *hudud* offenses.

The debate regarding the criminalization of apostasy appears to be ongoing in some of the surveyed countries. In Pakistan, a draft bill making apostasy by men a capital offense was proposed in 2007, but was not adopted. Similarly, in Iran a draft Penal Code containing a provision on apostasy was initially adopted by the country's Parliament in 2008, but ultimately rejected.

In some of the countries surveyed there is less clarity as to the status of apostasy as a crime. In Morocco, the Penal Code does not criminalize apostasy; however, the country's Supreme Council of Religious Scholars, the sole entity with constitutional authority to issue religious decrees, recently (in April 2013) decreed that apostasy is a capital offense. The legal status of this decree remains unclear. Although there is no statutory law criminalizing apostasy in Pakistan, some scholars believe that this gap could be filled by Sharia'a, which makes apostasy a capital offense.

In other countries, where formal laws do not criminalize apostasy, religious laws are used to prosecute persons for apostasy. Although Iran's current Penal Code does not criminalize it, courts have prosecuted individuals for apostasy based on their understanding of Sharia'a and legal opinions issued by religious leaders. In Jordan, where the Penal Code does not include specific provisions on apostasy, it is prosecuted in religious courts, including at the request of any member of the community.

In many of the jurisdictions surveyed, both those that impose criminal penalties for apostasy and those that do not, a finding of apostasy may have consequences related to matters of inheritance and the validity of the marital relationship of the individual concerned. For example, under Sharia'a, a Muslim spouse who converts to any other religion may not inherent from his/her Muslim relatives or spouse. Where a Muslim husband converts to another religion, his marriage is considered annulled under Islamic law.

Of the surveyed jurisdictions that do not expressly criminalize apostasy, many have laws that include broadly-worded provisions on insulting Islam or its Prophet and blasphemy, which could potentially be used to prosecute persons for apostasy. This category of countries includes Algeria, Bahrain, Indonesia, Iraq, Kuwait, Libya, Oman, and Syria. However, of the countries surveyed, Egypt is the only country known to have prosecuted apostasy in this manner. In 2007, a person who converted to Christianity was convicted under the country's blasphemy laws.

Although this aspect of the issue was not explored in detail in this report, researchers identified instances of extrajudicial punishment for apostasy. The surveys for Iran and Syria note that extrajudicial killings on the basis of allegations of apostasy have taken place in both countries at least once. Similarly, in Mauritania, where a journalist was arrested for apostasy in early 2014 for comments he published online, a local businessman offered a bounty to anyone who would kill the defendant.

Of the surveyed jurisdictions, Tunisia appears to be the only country that expressly prohibits extrajudicial punishment of individuals based on allegations of apostasy.

II. Country Surveys

Afghanistan

Under the Hanafi interpretation of Islamic law, as applied in Afghanistan, the crime of apostasy constitutes a *hudud* crime, a class of crimes that stipulates fixed punishments. Article 1 of the 1976 Afghan Penal Code states that *hudud* crimes must be punished in accordance with provisions of uncodified Islamic religious law as applied by Hanafi religious jurisprudence.[1] Similarly, article 130 of the Afghan Constitution states that while processing a case, courts must apply provisions of Hanafi jurisprudence if there is no provision in the Constitution or other laws regarding a specific case.[2] Prevailing Hanafi jurisprudence, as applied in Afghanistan, prescribes the death penalty for the crime of apostasy.[3] A person charged with apostasy can avoid prosecution and/or punishment if he recants.[4]

Convictions for apostasy could have wide-ranging consequences. Apostasy is considered a serious offense and persons so charged may "possibly face death by stoning, deprivation of all property and possessions, and/or the invalidation of their marriages."[5] However, it appears that prosecutions are rare. For instance, a Christian convert, Abdul Rahman, was accused of apostasy in 2006 but was apparently acquitted on a "technicality about his mental condition."[6] In late March 2006, he was granted asylum in Italy despite opposition to his release from the Afghan Parliament and members of the Muslim clergy in Afghanistan.[7] In 2011, Christian converts Said Musa and Shoaib Assadullah, who had been arrested for apostasy and faced potential death sentences, were released, reportedly as a result of international attention and diplomatic pressure.[8]

---

[1] PENAL CODE OF AFGHANISTAN art. 1, Issue No. 13, Serial No. 347 (Oct. 7, 1976), *available at* https://www.unodc. org/tldb/showDocument.do?documentUid=2100.

[2] CONSTITUTION OF AFGHANISTAN art. 130, Official Gazette No. 818 (Jan. 28, 2004), *available at* http://www.afghan -web.com/politics/current_constitution.html.

[3] Mandana Knust Rassekh Afshar, *The Case of an Afghan Apostate – The Right to a Fair Trial Between Islamic Law and Human Rights in the Afghan Constitution*, *in* 10 MAX PLANCK YEARBOOK OF UNITED NATIONS LAW 591–605 (Christiane E. Philipp ed., 2006), *available at* http://www.remep.mpg.de/files/student_body/knust-mandana/Knust_- _Case_of_an_Afghan_Apostate.pdf.

[4] U.S. DEPARTMENT OF STATE, BUREAU OF DEMOCRACY, HUMAN RIGHTS AND LABOR, INTERNATIONAL RELIGIOUS FREEDOM REPORT FOR 2012: AFGHANISTAN 3-4 (May 20, 2013), http://www.state.gov/documents/organization/ 208634.pdf.

[5] *Id.*

[6] Ron Synovitz, *Afghanistan: HRW Still Concerned About Apostasy Law*, RADIO FREE EUROPE/RADIO LIBERTY (Mar. 29, 2006), http://www.rferl.org/content/article/1067197.html.

[7] Elisabetta Povoledo, *Afghan Christian Convert Granted Asylum in Italy*, N.Y. TIMES (Mar. 29, 2006), http://www.nytimes.com/2006/03/29/international/asia/29cnd-afghan.html?_r=2&oref=slogin&.

[8] U.S. COMMISSION ON INTERNATIONAL RELIGIOUS FREEDOM (USCIRF), 2012 ANNUAL REPORT: AFGHANISTAN 7 (Mar. 2012), http://www.uscirf.gov/sites/default/files/resources/2012ARChapters/afghanistan%202012.pdf. *See also* Heidi Vogt & Adam Schreck, *Jailed Christian Convert Is Freed in Afghanistan*, WASHINGTON POST (Feb. 25, 2011), http://www. washingtonpost.com/wp-dyn/content/article/2011/02/25/AR2011022501007.html.

Algeria

Algerian law does not include a criminal offense of apostasy.[9] Offenses related to religion include article 144 bis(2) of the Penal Code, which provides that any individual who insults the prophet and the messengers of God, or denigrates the creed or prophets of Islam through writing, drawing, declaration, or any other means, will receive three to five years in prison, and/or be subject to a fine of between 50,000 and 100,000 Algerian dinars (approximately US$631 to $1263).[10] In addition, although Algeria permits religious organizations to participate in humanitarian works, it makes proselytizing by non-Muslims an offense punishable by a fine and up to five years' imprisonment.[11]

Bahrain

Article 309 of the Bahrain Penal Code of 1976 penalizes individuals who insult any religious sects with a term of imprisonment not exceeding one year or a fine not exceeding one hundred Bahraini dinars (approximately US$265).[12]

Brunei

Section 112(1) of the recently enacted Syariah (Sharia'a) Penal Code[13] of Brunei stipulates that a Muslim who declares himself non-Muslim is punishable with death, or with imprisonment for a term not exceeding thirty years and corporal punishment, depending on the type of evidence. If a Sharia'a Court is satisfied that the accused has repented, the Court must order an acquittal.[14] The Law was published in Brunei's official gazette on October 22, 2013, and will come into effect through a phased process. It appears that the death penalty for apostasy will be applied when the third phase of the Law goes into effect.[15] Corporal punishment will be applied twelve months after the Syariah Courts Criminal Procedure Code (CPC) is published in the gazette, and capital punishment will be applied twenty-four months after the CPC is published.[16]

---

[9] U.S. DEPARTMENT OF STATE, BUREAU OF DEMOCRACY, HUMAN RIGHTS AND LABOR, INTERNATIONAL RELIGIOUS FREEDOM REPORT FOR 2012: ALGERIA 5 (May 20, 2013), http://www.state.gov/documents/organization/208594.pdf.

[10] Law 15-66 of 1966, 8 June 1966, available on the official website of the Algerian Presidency of the Republic, http://www.joradp.dz/TRV/APenal.pdf (in Arabic).

[11] Law No. 02-06 (bis), *al Jarida al Rasmiyya*, vol.12, 1 March 2006.

[12] Law 15 of 1976, *al Jarida al Rasmiyya*, vol. 1170, 08 April 1976, http://www.legalaffairs.gov.bh/ AdvancedSearchDetails.aspx?id=4069#.U4SQNxChFyI (in Arabic).

[13] Syariah Penal Code Order, 2013, BRUNEI DARUSSALAM GOVERNMENT GAZETTE (Oct. 22, 2013), http://www. agc.gov.bn/agc1/images/LAWS/Gazette_PDF/2013/EN/syariah%20penal%20code%20order2013.pdf.

[14] *Id.* § 117.

[15] *Syariah Penal Code Order Declaration Ceremony – April 30, 2014*, BRUNEI TIMES (Apr. 30, 2014), http://www. bt.com.bn/frontpage-bookmarks-news-national/2014/04/30/syariah-penal-code-order-declaration-ceremony-april-30.

[16] Rabiatul Kamit & Bandar Seri Begawan, *Kedah Officials in Brunei to Observe Syariah Law*, BRUNEI TIMES (May 16, 2014), http://www.bt.com.bn/frontpage-news-national/2014/05/16/kedah-officials-brunei-observe-syariah-law. *See also Syariah Panel Code Briefing for Military Personnel*, MINISTRY OF DEFENSE BRUNEI DARUSSALAM (Apr. 10, 2014), http://www2.mindef.gov.bn/MOD_Brunei/index.php/news-archives-mainmenu-70/2310-syariah-panel-code-briefing-for-military-personnel.

Egypt

While Egypt does not have a statutory ban on apostasy, article 98(f) of Egypt's Penal Code, as amended by Law 147/2006, states that "whoever makes use of religion in propagating, either by words, in writing, or in any other means, extreme ideas for the purpose of inciting strife, ridiculing or insulting a heavenly religion or a sect following it, or damaging national unity" is punishable with six months to five years' imprisonment, and/or a fine of five hundred to one thousand Egyptian pounds (approximately US$71 to $142).[17]

Concerning the prosecution of apostasy cases, in 1996, the Egyptian Court of Cassation reportedly ruled that the writings of Muslim scholar Nasr Abu Zayd were an act of apostasy. Accordingly, based on the Court's decision, his marriage was declared void.[18] In addition, news reports indicate that in May 2007, Bahaa El-Din El-Akkad, a former Egyptian Muslim and member of Tabligh and Daawa (an organization to spread Islam), was imprisoned for two years under the charge of "blasphemy against Islam" after converting to Christianity.[19]

Indonesia

Indonesia does not have a law specifically devoted to apostasy, but punishment for acts of blasphemy is prescribed in article 156(a) of the Penal Code. The Code imposes a penalty of up to five years' imprisonment for expressions or actions in public that have "the character of being at enmity with, abusing or staining a religion, adhered to in Indonesia" or are committed "with the intention to prevent a person to adhere [sic] to any religion based on the belief of the almighty God."[20]

Either the Penal Code or a 1965 Presidential Decision on blasphemy could be used to prosecute someone for renouncing his or her religion.[21] This Decision specifically forbids

> every individual . . . in public from intentionally conveying, endorsing or attempting to
> gain public support in the interpretation of a certain religion embraced by the people of
> Indonesia or undertaking religious based activities that resemble the religious activities of

---

[17] Law 58 of 1937 (Criminal Code of 1937), art. 98(f), *available at* http://www.mohamoon-montada.com/Default. aspx?action=ArabicLaw&ID=20 (in Arabic).

[18] *See* Maurits S. Berger, *Apostasy and Public Policy in Contemporary Egypt: An Evaluation of Recent Cases from Egypt's Highest Courts*, 25 HUM. RTS. Q. 720 (2003), *available at* https://openaccess.leidenuniv.nl/bitstream/handle/1887/13673/MS%20Berger%20-%20Apostasy%20 and%20public%20policy%20in%20contemporary%20Egypt.pdf?sequence=1.

[19] *Former Muslim Sheikh Imprisoned for Insulting Islam Freed*, ADVOCATES FOR THE PERSECUTED (Aug. 18, 2011), http://advocatesforthepersecuted.org/index.php/stories/3045.html (quoting Compass Direct News).

[20] Law No. 27 of 1999, Penal Code of Indonesia (May 19, 1999), art. 156(a), ¶¶ a & b, available on the World Intellectual Property Organization (WIPO) website, *at* http://www.wipo.int/wipolex/en/text.jsp?file_id=181078.

[21] Penetapan Presiden Republik Indonesia Nomor 1 Tahun 1965 Tentang Pencegahan Penyalahgunaan Dan/Atau Penodaan Agama [Presidential Decision No. 1 of 1965 on Preventing Abuse or Defamation of Religion], http://www.dpr.go.id/id/undang-undang/1965/1/uu/PENCEGAHAN-PENYALAHGUNAAN-DAN-ATAU-PENODAAN-AGAMA.

the religion in question, where such interpretation and activities are in deviation of the basic teachings of the religion.[22]

This law, which recognizes six official religions (Islam, Catholicism, Protestantism, Buddhism, Hinduism, and Confucianism), allows the government to ban groups and prosecute people who "distort" any of these religions.[23] Violation of this law carries a maximum penalty of five years of imprisonment.[24] The 1965 blasphemy law was upheld by the country's Constitutional Court in 2010, with the Court holding that "the government maintains the power to impose limitations on religious freedoms based up on security considerations."[25]

In addition to the blasphemy laws, Indonesia also has in place a targeted ban on proselytizing. In 2008, the government issued a ministerial decree specifically banning the Ahmadiyya Muslim Community from proselytizing.[26]

Reports indicate an increase in the application of blasphemy laws in Indonesia in recent years. While close to 40 individuals have been convicted on blasphemy charges since 1965, over half of the convictions were after 2009 with four convictions in 2011 and ten in 2012.[27]

---

[22] *Id.* art. 1, *translated in* JO-ANNE PRUD'HOMME, FREEDOM HOUSE, POLICING BELIEF: THE IMPACT OF BLASPHEMY LAWS ON HUMAN RIGHTS 46 (Oct. 2010), http://www.freedomhouse.org/sites/default/files/PolicingBelief_Indonesia.pdf.

[23] *See* Kelly Buchanan, *Indonesia: Constitutional Court Upholds Blasphemy Law,* GLOBAL LEGAL MONITOR (Apr. 22, 2010), http://www.loc.gov/lawweb/servlet/lloc_news?disp3_l205401941_text.

[24] *Id.*

[25] U.S. DEPARTMENT OF STATE, BUREAU OF DEMOCRACY, HUMAN RIGHTS AND LABOR, INTERNATIONAL RELIGIOUS FREEDOM REPORT FOR 2012: INDONESIA 4 (May 20, 2013), http://www.state.gov/documents/organization/208444.pdf.

[26] *Id.* at 3.

[27] *Id.* at 8.

Iran

Iran's current Penal Code, which was approved by the country's Guardian Council on January 18, 2012,[28] does not include provisions criminalizing apostasy. However, a draft form of the Code containing several provisions on apostasy had been approved by the Iranian Parliament in principal on September 9, 2008, but was not subsequently adopted.[29] While Iranian law does not provide for the death penalty for apostasy, the courts can hand down that punishment, and have done so in previous years, based on their interpretation of Sharia'a law and *fatwas* (legal opinions or decrees issued by Islamic religious leaders).[30]

In September 2012, Christian pastor Youcef Nadarkhani was acquitted of charges of apostasy brought against him in 2010 that carried the death sentence. Nadarkhani was instead convicted of evangelizing Muslims and given a three-year sentence.[31] Reportedly, the last convert to Christianity in Iran to be judicially convicted of apostasy and sentenced to death was Mehdi Dibaj in 1994, although the sentence was not carried out.[32] The European Centre for Law and Justice has pointed out, however, that "this absence of recent punishment does not mean that there was no execution of converts, within or outside the judicial system. For example, Mehdi Dibaj and other Protestant pastors have been brutally murdered outside of the court system."[33]

---

[28] MOHAMMAD HOSSEIN NAYYERI, NEW ISLAMIC PENAL CODE OF THE ISLAMIC REPUBLIC OF IRAN: AN OVERVIEW 4 (University of Essex Research Paper Series, Mar. 31, 2012), http://www.iranhrdc.org/english/human-rights-documents/ngo-reports/university-of-essex-university-of-essex-iran-unit/1000000159-new-islamic-penal-code-of-the-islamic-republic-of-iran-an-overview.html. "The Guardian Council [is] a politically influential twelve member body which includes six clergy members who are mandated and appointed by the Supreme Leader of the IRI [Islamic Republic of Iran]." *Id.* at 1–2.

[29] Wahied Wahdat-Hagh, *Iran's Barbaric New Laws*, THE COMMENTATOR (June 7, 2013), http://www.thecommentator.com/article/3736/iran_s_barbaric_new_laws. For the text of the draft provisions, see *Iran's New Apostasy Law: New Penal Code Mandates Death for Converts*, IRANIAN CHRISTIANS FOR RELIGIOUS FREEDOM, http://www.madeye18.com/index.php?option=com_content&view=article&id=97:irans-new-apostasy-law&catid=31:news-english&Itemid=62 (last visited May 27, 2014).

[30] U.S. DEPARTMENT OF STATE, BUREAU OF DEMOCRACY, HUMAN RIGHTS AND LABOR, 2013 HUMAN RIGHTS REPORTS: IRAN (Feb. 27, 2014), http://www.state.gov/j/drl/rls/hrrpt/2013/nea/220352.htm; EUROPEAN CENTRE FOR LAW AND JUSTICE, WRITTEN OBSERVATIONS OF THE EUROPEAN CENTRE FOR LAW AND JUSTICE (Apr. 13, 2009), http://eclj.org/pdf/eclj_iran_amicusbriefrbgmbvturkey_090416.pdf.

[31] U.S. DEPARTMENT OF STATE, BUREAU OF DEMOCRACY, HUMAN RIGHTS AND LABOR, INTERNATIONAL RELIGIOUS FREEDOM REPORT FOR 2012: IRAN (May 20, 2013), http://www.state.gov/j/drl/rls/irf/religiousfreedom/index.htm?year=2012&dlid=208388%20.

[32] EUROPEAN CENTRE FOR LAW AND JUSTICE, *supra* note 30 (citing *Iran: Death Penalty Proposed for 'Apostates,'* COMPASS DIRECT NEWS (Feb. 8, 2008), https://www.worldwatchmonitor.org/2008/02-February/newsarticle_5231.html/, which noted that the sentence was dropped and Dibaj released because of international pressure, *and* U.S. DEPARTMENT OF STATE, INTERNATIONAL RELIGIOUS FREEDOM REPORT 2008: IRAN § II, Legal/Policy Framework (Sept. 19, 2008), http://www.state.gov/g/drl/rls/irf/2008/108482.htm, which stated that there were "no reported cases of the death penalty being applied for apostasy during the reporting period [2008].").

[33] EUROPEAN CENTRE FOR LAW AND JUSTICE, *supra* note 30, citing to *Iran: Death Penalty Proposed for 'Apostates.'*

According to the US Department of State, the last death penalty for apostasy that was actually carried out occurred in 1990.[34] The US Department of State pointed out in a report issued in 2009 that the death penalty can be imposed on the basis of ambiguous charges, such as "'attempts against the security of the state,' 'outrage against high-ranking officials,' and 'insults against the memory of Imam Khomeini and against the Supreme Leader of the Islamic Republic,'" and that

> although there were few details, the government arrested, convicted, and executed persons on questionable criminal charges, including drug trafficking, when their actual "offenses" were political. The government charged members of religious minorities with crimes such as "confronting the regime" and apostasy, and conducted trials in these cases in the same manner as it would treat threats to national security.[35]

Iraq

Article 372 of Iraq's Penal Code of 1969 provides that any individual who insults the creed of a religious sect or its practices, or publicly insults a symbol or person that is an object of sanctification, worship, or reverence for a religious sect, may be punished with a term of imprisonment not exceeding three years or a fine not exceeding 300 Iraqi dinars (approximately US$0.25).[36]

Jordan

While there is no express statutory prohibition on apostasy, conversion trials are heard by Islamic courts and may be instituted by any member of the community.[37] According to Islamic law, there are consequences when Muslims adopt religions other than Islam. For instance, if someone is convicted of apostasy, the Islamic courts adjudicating matters of personal status have the power to void the person's marriage and deny his/her right to inherit from a spouse and from Muslim relatives.[38]

---

[34] Press Release, Victoria Nuland, Spokesperson, U.S. Department of State, Persecution of Religious Minorities in Iran (July 6, 2011), http://www.state.gov/r/pa/prs/ps/2011/07/167733.htm.

[35] U.S. DEPARTMENT OF STATE, BUREAU OF DEMOCRACY, HUMAN RIGHTS AND LABOR, 2008 HUMAN RIGHTS REPORT: IRAN (Feb. 25, 2009), http://www.state.gov/j/drl/rls/hrrpt/2008/nea/119115.htm.

[36] Law 111-1969, al Jarida al Rasmiyya, vol. 1778, 15 December 1969, available at http://www.iraqld.com/LoadLawBook.aspx?SP=IDX&SC=120120012516407&Year=1969&PageNum=1 (in Arabic).

[37] Id. According to a report by a law firm in Jordan, the concept of penalizing apostasy was confirmed by a decision of the Jordan Cassation Court in Case No. 3574/2005. The principle that an apostasy case can be filed before the Sharia'a Court by any Muslim person against individuals who might be suspected of committing acts of apostasy was verified by a decision issued by the Sharia'a Court on June 30, 1997, in Case No. 1136/43107. Tarik Arida, Apostate from Islam in Jordan, ARIDA LAW FIRM, available at http://www.hg.org/article.asp?id=22836 (last visited May 27, 2014).

[38] Id.

A person could also be subjected to accusations of apostasy with all its consequences for activities other than conversion. In one reported case from 2010, Jordanian poet Islam Samhan was accused of apostasy for poems he wrote.[39]

In addition, Jordan explicitly criminalizes blasphemy. Article 273 of Jordan's Penal Code of 1960 punishes any individual who insults the Prophet Mohamed with a term of imprisonment of one to three years.[40]

Kuwait

According to Law 51 of 1984 on Personal Status, which is based on Islamic Sharia'a, under article 18, the marriage of a non-Muslim man to a Muslim woman is considered annulled. Article 145 of the aforementioned law applies such legal and religious principle to Muslim husbands that might adopt other religions than Islam during the marital relationship. Moreover, under article 294 of this law, an apostate is not able to inherent from his Muslim relatives or marital spouse.[41]

Kuwait also has laws that could be used to punish individuals who are accused of blasphemy. Law 19 of 2012 on National Unity was issued to amend article 111 of the Penal Code by imposing harsher penalties and criminalizing any publications and broadcasting content that could be considered offensive to religious "sects" or groups, including through social media. The new law punishes such crimes with a fine ranging from US$36,000 to US$720,000 and a maximum of seven years in prison. [42]

Like its apostasy laws, the country's laws on blasphemy permit anyone to file criminal charges against an author of any material that the person believes to be defamatory to a religious group.[43]

Lebanon

The Lebanese Penal Code punishes individuals who perform acts that are considered blasphemous to the name of God.[44] It also imposes penalties against individuals who publicly insult the religious proceedings of any religion.[45]

---

[39] Tom A. Peter, *A Poet Faces Death for "Killing" God*, GLOBAL POST (Jan. 2, 2010; updated May 30, 2010), http://www.globalpost.com/dispatch/jordan/090922/jordanian-poet-trial-apostacy.

[40] Law 16 of 1960, *al Jarida al Rasmiyya*, vol. 1487, 1 January 1960, p. 374.

[41] Law 51 of 1984, 23 July 1984, available on the Gulf Cooperation Council Legal Network website, *at* http://www.gcc-legal.org/MojPortalPublic/DisplayLegislations.aspx?country=1&LawTreeSectionID=1427 (last visited June 2, 2014).

[42] Law 19 of 2012, *al Jarida al Rasmiyya*, vol. 1102, 21 October 2012, *available at* http://www.kuna.net.kw/ArticleDetails.aspx?id=2269659&language=ar (in Arabic).

[43] *Id.*

[44] Law 340 of 1943, 1 March 1943, art. 273, available on the World Intellectual Property Organization (WIPO) website, *at* http://www.wipo.int/wipolex/en/text.jsp?file_id=243255 (in Arabic).

[45] *Id.* art. 274.

Libya

While Libyan law does not expressly criminalize apostasy, there is a legal instrument that bans blasphemy. Article 291 (Insult of the State Religion) of Libya's Penal Code of 1953 provides as follows:

> Whoever publicly abuses the Islamic religion—that being the official religion of the State under the Libyan Constitution—with verbal terms not befitting for the Divine Being, the Messenger, or the Prophets, shall be punished with imprisonment for a term not exceeding two years.[46]

Mauritania

Apostasy is punished under article 306 of the Mauritanian Criminal Code.[47] This article provides that "[a]ny Muslim guilty of the crime of apostasy" is to be given the opportunity to repent within three days. If the accused does not repent within that period, he/she is to be sentenced to death, and all of his/her property shall be confiscated by the government.[48] It appears that article 306 of the Criminal Code also provides that if a person who has been sentenced to death for apostasy repents before his/her execution, the Mauritanian Supreme Court can commute his/her death sentence to a jail sentence of between three months and two years, and a fine of UM5,000–60,000 (approximately US$17–$203).[49]

A young Mauritanian journalist was arrested for apostasy on January 2, 2014, for having posted a text online that was seen as blasphemous.[50] This case has generated a public outcry. Protesters called for the man's execution, a local businessman declared that he was willing to pay a reward to anyone who killed the journalist,[51] and even the National Human Rights Commission of Mauritania condemned the writings that triggered the arrest.[52]

---

[46] Penal Code of 1953 art. 291, available on the official website of the Libyan Ministry of Justice, http://www.aladel.gov.ly/main/modules/sections/item.php?itemid=68 (in Arabic; translation by author).

[47] Ordonnance 83-162 du 9 juillet 1983 portant institution d'un Code Pénal (Ordinance 83-162 of July 9, 1983, Establishing a Criminal Code) (July 9, 1983), art. 306, JOURNAL OFFICIEL DE LA RÉPUBLIQUE ISLAMIQUE DE MAURITANIE [OFFICIAL GAZETTE OF THE ISLAMIC REPUBLIC OF MAURITANIA], Feb. 29, 1984, *available at* http://www.droit-afrique.com/images/textes/ Mauritanie/Mauritanie%20-%20Code%20penal.pdf.

[48] *Id.* (translation by author).

[49] *Id.*

[50] Jemal Oumar, *Mauritanians Condemn Call to Kill Author* (Jan. 10, 2014), ALLAFRICA, http://allafrica.com/ stories/201401120133.html.

[51] *Id.*

[52] Communiqué from Irabiha Abdel Wedoud, Présidente de la Commission Nationale des Droits de l'Homme [CNDH] Mauritanie [President of the National Human Rights Commission of Mauritania], Communiqué de la CNDH sur les propos blasphématoires tenus à l'encontre du prophète (PSL) [Communiqué of the CNDH on the Blasphemous Remarks Made Against the Prophet (PBUH)] (Jan. 7, 2014), *available at* http://www.cridem.org/C_ Info.php?article=651667.

Morocco

Morocco does not impose the death penalty against apostates under the provisions of its Penal Code. However, in April 2013, the Supreme Council of Religious Scholars issued a religious decree (*fatwa*) that Moroccan Muslims who leave Islam must be sentenced to death.[53] Religious decrees are significant because Islam is the official state religion under article 3 of the Moroccan Constitution of 2011.[54] Additionally, under article 41 of the Constitution, the Supreme Council of Religious Scholars "is the sole instance enabled [*habilitée*] to comment [*prononcer*] on religious consultations (Fatwas)."[55]

Oman

Oman has a legal instrument that could be used to punish both blasphemy and apostasy. Article 209 of Oman's Penal Code punishes with a term of imprisonment of between ten days and three years, or a fine between five to five hundred Omani Riyals (approximately US$13 to $1,300) an individual who commits the following acts: (1) publicly blasphemes God or the prophet Mohamed, (2) commits an affront to religions and faiths by spoken or written word, or (3) breaches the peace of a lawful religious gathering.[56]

Under Law 32 of 1997 on Personal Status, rules of Islamic Sharia'a on matters concerning inheritance and the validity of the marriage of a non-Muslim spouse apply.[57]

Pakistan

There is no specific statutory law that criminalizes apostasy in Pakistan. In 2007, a bill to impose the death penalty for apostasy for males and life imprisonment for females was proposed in Parliament but failed to pass.[58] Nevertheless, some scholars believe that the principle that "a lacuna in the statute law was to be filled with reference to Islamic law"[59] could potentially apply to the crime of apostasy.

Although no examples of anyone actually being criminally prosecuted for apostasy were found, conversion is not without consequence. It has been reported that if a married Muslim couple

---

[53] *Fatwa (Religious Decree) to Kill Apostates Sparks Fierce Controversy in Morocco*, MIDDLE EAST ONLINE (Apr. 18, 2013), http://www.middle-east-online.com/english/?id=58230.

[54] MOROCCAN CONSTITUTION OF 2011, unofficial English translation *in* WORLD CONSTITUTIONS ILLUSTRATED: MOROCCO (Jefri Jay Ruchti ed. & trans., 2011), *available at* http://www.constitutionnet.org/files/morocco_eng.pdf.

[55] *Id.* art. 41 (wording per *World Constitutions* translation).

[56] Royal Decree 7-1974, *al Jarida al Rasmiyya*, 26 February 1974, available on the website of the Omani Government, http://www.rop.gov.om/pdfs/roplaws/arabic/ROPRULE-1.pdf (in Arabic).

[57] Law 32 of 1997, *al Jarida al Rasmiyya,* vol. 601, 4 June 1997.

[58] Bilal Farooqi, *Being Pakistani and Atheist a Dangerous Combo, but Some Ready to Brave It*, PAKISTAN TODAY (Sept. 17, 2011), http://www.pakistantoday.com.pk/2011/09/17/city/karachi/being-pakistani-and-atheist-a-dangerous-combo-but-some-ready-to-brave-it/.

[59] MARTIN LAU, THE ROLE OF ISLAM IN THE LEGAL SYSTEM OF PAKISTAN 137 (2006).

converts to another religion, the couple's children become illegitimate and may become wards of the State.[60] In addition, according to one report, though it is theoretically possible to change one's religion from Islam, in practice, the state attempts to hinder the process.[61] Converts from Islam and atheists may also be vulnerable to Pakistan's blasphemy law, which prescribes life imprisonment for desecrating or defiling the Quran and the death sentence to anyone for using derogatory remarks towards the Prophet Mohamed.[62] In 1990, a Christian convert who was accused of insulting the Prophet was denied bail by a Sessions Court and an Appeals Division of the Lahore High Court on the basis that his conversion from Islam to Christianity was a cognizable offense, even though there was no such specific offense in Pakistan's Penal Code.[63]

Qatar

Qatar's Law 11 of 2004 incorporates the traditional punishments of Islamic law for various offenses, including apostasy. Article 1 of the Law states that

> the provisions of Islamic law for the following offenses are applied if the defendant or victim is a Muslim:
> 1. The *hudud* offenses related to theft, banditry, adultery, defamation, alcohol consumption, and apostasy.
> 2. The offenses of retaliation (*qisas*) and blood money (*diyah*).[64]

While apostasy is one of the offenses subject to the death penalty, Qatar has not imposed any penalty for this offense since its independence in 1971.[65]

Qatar also criminalizes proselytizing. Under article 257, any individual who establishes an organization to proselytize may be punished with a term of imprisonment of up to seven years.[66]

---

[60] U.S. DEPARTMENT OF STATE, BUREAU OF DEMOCRACY, HUMAN RIGHTS AND LABOR, INTERNATIONAL RELIGIOUS FREEDOM REPORT FOR 2012: PAKISTAN 7 (May 20, 2013), http://www.state.gov/documents/organization/208650.pdf.

[61] Immigration and Refugee Board of Canada, *Pakistan: Religious Conversion, Including Treatment of Converts and Forced Conversions (2009-2012)* (Jan. 14, 2013), available on the United Nations High Commissioner for Refugees (UNHCR) portal, *at* http://www.refworld.org/docid/510f8b832.html.

[62] "Offences relating to religion" are provisioned under sections 295–298-C of the Pakistan Penal Code Act No. XLV of 1860, *available at* http://www.refworld.org/docid/485231942.html.

[63] Amnesty International, *Use and Abuse of the Blasphemy Laws*, ASA/33/08/94 (July 1, 1994), *available at* http://www.refworld.org/docid/3ae6a9aa4.html.

[64] Law 11-2004, *al Jarida al Rasmiyya* vol. 7, 30 May 2004, p. 53, *available at* http://www.almeezan.qa/LawArticles.aspx?LawArticleID=593&LawId=26&language=en (in English translation).

[65] U.S. DEPARTMENT OF STATE, BUREAU OF DEMOCRACY, HUMAN RIGHTS AND LABOR, INTERNATIONAL RELIGIOUS FREEDOM REPORT FOR 2012: QATAR 2 (May 20, 2013), http://www.state.gov/documents/organization/208620.pdf.

[66] Law 11-2004, art. 257.

Saudi Arabia

Islamic Sharia'a is the law of the land in Saudi Arabia. The country has no penal code. One of the main sources of Islamic law is the *hadith* or ascribed sayings of the Prophet Mohamed. Islamic law imposes the death penalty on apostates based on the following statements attributed to the Prophet Mohamed in some *hadith* collections:

> (1) "If somebody (a Muslim) discards his religion, kill him[,]"[67] and
> (2) "The blood of a Muslim who confesses that none has the right to be worshipped but Allah and that I am His Apostle, cannot be shed except in three cases: In Qisas for murder, a married person who commits illegal sexual intercourse and the one who reverts from Islam and leaves the Muslims."[68]

It appears that apostasy is understood to be more than mere conversion and the law against it is actively enforced. For instance, in 2012 Saudi authorities charged Hamza Kashgari, a Saudi writer, with apostasy based on comments he made on Twitter expressing his personal religious views.[69] Although he initially fled the country, he was detained in Malaysia and extradited to Saudi Arabia where, after having repented, he was placed in protective custody.[70] In another incident, Saudi authorities detained two men and charged them with apostasy for adopting the Ahmadiyya interpretation of Islam.[71]

Sudan

Article 126 of the Sudanese Penal Code, on apostasy, provides that any Muslim who declares publicly that he/she has adopted any religion other than Islam commits the crime of apostasy and is punishable with the death penalty. However, the provision waives the death penalty if the convicted person reconverts to Islam.[72]

The ban on apostasy, an offense subject to private prosecution, appears to be actively enforced. In a recent case, a First Instance Court in the Sudanese capital, Khartoum, convicted a Christian woman, Meriam Ibrahim, against whom apostasy charges were filed by her own family members, of adultery and apostasy. She was sentenced to one hundred lashes and the death by

---

[67] SAHIH BUKHARI, vol. 4, book 52, No. 260, *available at* http://www.usc.edu/org/cmje/religious-texts/hadith/bukhari/052-sbt.php#004.052.260.

[68] *Id.* vol. 9, book 83, No. 17, *available at* http://www.usc.edu/org/cmje/religious-texts/hadith/bukhari/083-sbt.php#009.083.017.

[69] *Saudi Arabia: Writer Faces Apostasy Trial*, HUMAN RIGHTS WATCH (Feb. 13, 2012), http://www.hrw.org/news/2012/02/13/saudi-arabia-writer-faces-apostasy-trial.

[70] U.S. DEPARTMENT OF STATE, BUREAU OF DEMOCRACY, HUMAN RIGHTS AND LABOR, INTERNATIONAL RELIGIOUS FREEDOM REPORT FOR 2012: SAUDI ARABIA 9 (May 20, 2013), http://www.state.gov/documents/organization/208622.pdf.

[71] *Saudi Arabia: 2 Years Behind Bars on Apostasy Accusation*, HUMAN RIGHTS WATCH (May 15, 2014), http://www.hrw.org/news/2014/05/15/saudi-arabia-2-years-behind-bars-apostasy-accusation.

[72] SUDAN PENAL CODE OF 1991 art. 126(1)–(3), *available at* http://www.wipo.int/wipolex/en/text.jsp?file_id=241802 (in Arabic).

hanging.[73] The Court then suspended the implementation of the verdict for two years so that Ibrahim, who was pregnant at the time, could give birth and nurse her child for two years.[74] However, on May 31, 2014, it was reported that the Sudanese authorities, following intense international pressure, agreed to free Ibrahim.[75]

Syria

Syria's Penal Code provides in article 462 that individuals who publicly defame religious proceedings are punishable with a term of two years' imprisonment.[76]

Islamist extremist groups in Syria have applied extrajudicial penalties against individuals who are accused of apostasy. For instance, in November 2013, an al Qaeda-linked group (The Islamic State of Iraq and Levant) executed a man after accusing him of apostasy and insulting God.[77]

Tunisia

Tunisia not only eschews the death penalty for apostasy, but in article 6 of the Tunisian Constitution of 2014 also protects its citizens by preventing any attacks against them based on accusations of apostasy.[78]

United Arab Emirates

The United Arab Emirates criminalizes apostasy through the incorporation of the concept of *hudud* crimes under Islamic Sharia'a into its Penal Code. Those crimes include adultery, apostasy, murder, theft, highway robbery that involves killing, and a false accusation of committing adultery. Article 1 of the Penal Code provides that Islamic law applies to *hudud* crimes, the acceptance of blood money, and homicide.[79] In addition, article 66 states that among the "original punishments" under the law are the punishments of *hudud* crimes, including by

---

[73] *Death Penalty Against a Sudanese Woman for Adopting Christianity*, ELAPH (May 15, 2014), http://www.elaph. com/Web/News/2014/5/904435.html (in Arabic); EMBASSY OF THE REPUBLIC OF THE SUDAN, WASHINGTON D.C., The Case of Mariam Is neither Religious Nor Political, It is Legal 1 (May 21, 2014) (copy with GLRC staff).

[74] *Meriam Ibrahim: Sudan 'to Free' Death Row Woman*, BBC NEWS AFRICA (May 31, 2014), http://www.bbc.com/news/world-africa-27651483.

[75] *Id.*

[76] Law 148 of 1949, available on the official website of the Syrian Parliament, http://parliament.sy/forms/uploads/ laws/Decree/1949/penal_18.htm (in Arabic).

[77] *Al Qaeda Cuts off Head of Rebel Battalion in Syria*, AL ALALAM (Nov. 27, 2013), http://en.alalam.ir/news/1538609.

[78] Tunisia Constitution of 2014, unofficial English translation *available at* http://www.tunisia-live.net/2014/01/ 21/tunisias-draft-constitution-an-english-translation/.

[79] Law 3 of 1987, *al Jarida al Rasmiyya*, vol. 182, 8 December 1987, *available at* http://www.gcc-legal.org/MojPortalPublic/DisplayLegislations.aspx?country=2&LawTreeSectionID=3947 (in Arabic).

imposing the death penalty.[80]   However, "there have been no known prosecutions or legal punishments for apostasy in court."[81]

Yemen

The crime of apostasy may be subject to the death penalty by virtue of article 12 of the Yemen Penal Code of 1994, as amended by Law 24 of 2006, which identifies crimes, including apostasy, that are punished according to the provisions of Islamic Sharia'a.[82]   Furthermore, article 259 provides that individuals committing the act of apostasy may be punished with the death penalty.[83]   It also waives the punishment for apostasy if the individual repents and returns to Islam and denounces his new faith.

Anti-apostasy laws are enforced. In November 2012, Yemeni citizen Ali Qasim Al-Saeedi was arrested by the authorities and charged with apostasy for posting articles and research on his personal Facebook account that questioned the teachings of the Quran.[84]   However, it has been reported that Yemen does not enforce the death penalty for apostasy.[85]

---

[80] *Id.* art. 66.

[81] U.S. DEPARTMENT OF STATE, BUREAU OF DEMOCRACY, HUMAN RIGHTS AND LABOR, INTERNATIONAL RELIGIOUS FREEDOM REPORT FOR 2012: UNITED ARAB EMIRATES 3 (May 20, 2013), http://www.state.gov/documents/organization/208628.pdf.

[82] Presidential Decree of Law 12-1994, published on the official website of the former President of Yemen *at* http://www.presidentsaleh.gov.ye/showlaws.php?_lwbkno=2&_lwptno=1&_lwnmid=243 (in Arabic).

[83] *Id.* art. 259.

[84] Nadia Haddash, *Family of Yemeni Blogger Prosecuted for Apostasy Calls Accusations 'Unacceptable'*, YEMEN TIMES (Dec. 6, 2012), http://www.yementimes.com/en/1631/report/1701/Family-of-Yemeni-blogger-prosecuted-for-apostasy-calls-accusations-%27unacceptable%27.htm.

[85] U.S. DEPARTMENT OF STATE, BUREAU OF DEMOCRACY, HUMAN RIGHTS AND LABOR, INTERNATIONAL RELIGIOUS FREEDOM REPORT FOR 2012: YEMEN 2 (May 20, 2013), http://www.state.gov/documents/organization/208632.pdf.